Today's Superstars
Entertainment

Jim Carrey

by Amy Stone

Gareth Stevens
Publishing

Please visit our web site at: www.garethstevens.com
For a free color catalog describing Gareth Stevens Publishing's
list of high-quality books, call 1-800-542-2595 (USA) or
1-800-387-3178 (Canada).

Library of Congress Cataloging-in-Publication Data

Stone, Amy, 1947-
    Jim Carrey / Amy Stone.
        p. cm. — (Today's Superstars: Entertainment)
    Includes bibliographical references and index.
    ISBN: 978-0-8368-8197-4 (lib. bdg.)
    1. Carrey, Jim, 1962- —Juvenile literature. 2. Motion picture actors and
actresses—United States—Biography—Juvenile literature. 3. Comedians—
United States—Biography—Juvenile literature. I. Title.
PN2287.C278S76   2008
791.4302'8092—dc22   2007017325

This edition first published in 2008 by
Gareth Stevens Publishing
A Weekly Reader® Company
1 Reader's Digest Road
Pleasantville, NY 10570-7000 USA

Copyright © 2008 by Gareth Stevens, Inc.

Editor: Gini Holland
Art direction and design: Tammy West
Picture research: Diane Laska-Swanke
Production: Jessica Yanke

Photo credits: Cover, The Everett Collection; pp. 5, 8, 23 © Universal/courtesy
Everett Collection; p. 7 © NBC/courtesy Everett Collection; pp. 11, 15, 24
© AP Images; pp. 17, 19 © 20th Century Fox Film Corp./courtesy Everett
Collection; p. 18 © MTM/courtesy Everett Collection; pp. 21, 27 © New Line
Cinema/courtesy Everett Collection; p. 22 © Richard Perry/CORBIS SYGMA;
p. 26 © Paramount/courtesy Everett Collection

Printed in the United States of America

1 2 3 4 5 6 7 8 9 11 10 09 08 07

Contents

Chapter 1

The Power of Comedy

Jim Carrey stares at the bowl of tomato soup in front of him. Then he stretches his hands out above the bowl. He rolls his eyes upward. Jim opens his mouth wide enough to show every tooth. Without touching the bowl, Jim makes waves in the soup by sending "power" from his hands. As star of the movie *Bruce Almighty,* Jim Carrey is playing Bruce Nolan. Bruce is an ordinary man. But God has decided Bruce can play God — for a while. In the soup scene, Bruce's hands hold as much power as God's.

Roles such as this have defined Jim Carrey's comedy film career. By stretching his face muscles every which way, Jim makes his characters funny. He also makes them easy to remember. He puts intense energy into these parts. Jim's skills and talents have helped him become a highly successful film comic. He doesn't really have godlike powers. But he sure has the power to make people laugh.

Like many a superstar, Jim Carrey did not turn into a star overnight. In fact, he

In *Bruce Almighty*, Jim uses his god-like hands to part the "red sea" of his tomato soup. He uses his facial expressions to make the scene funny.

didn't even start his career as an actor. He began as a stand-up comedian. In his late teens and early twenties, he performed in comedy clubs throughout Canada, where he was born, and in Los Angeles, California. Jim's comedy routine included impressions. He pretended to be such famous performers as Elvis Presley, Sammy Davis Jr., and Kermit the Frog. To do an impression, a comic copies someone's voice, facial expressions, gestures, and body movements.

Jim Carrey did all that — and more. He captured the key emotions that defined the person. Audiences loved his amazing impressions. Many people found them magical. Fans could almost believe that the character had come to life.

Becoming the Grinch

It took hard work — and a bit of luck — but Jim did it. After starting out as a locally known stand-up comic, he became a nationally known movie star. Jim Carrey has starred in more than sixteen films. Together, his films have earned more than $2 billion in box office sales. He can play all sorts of roles. He has starred in goofy and gross comedies such as *Dumb and Dumber* and *Liar Liar*. But he has also played dramatic roles in such movies as *The Truman Show* and *Man on the Moon*. Carrey has shown range as an actor. He has even become Dr. Seuss' famous creature, the Grinch, in the 2000 film *How The Grinch Stole Christmas*.

How The Grinch Stole Christmas was based on a 1957 children's book of the

The Lonely Life of a Stand-up Comic

Actor and comedian Will Ferrell has called the life of a stand-up comic both hard and lonely. The comic stands directly in front of a live audience. All alone. He or she talks with the audience, telling fast-paced jokes and funny stories. Sometimes, the comic does an impression of a famous performer. The comic's goal is to make the audience laugh. Plus, the comic wants the audience's respect. A comic doesn't always get it. Audiences sometimes boo or yell insults when they don't like the jokes.

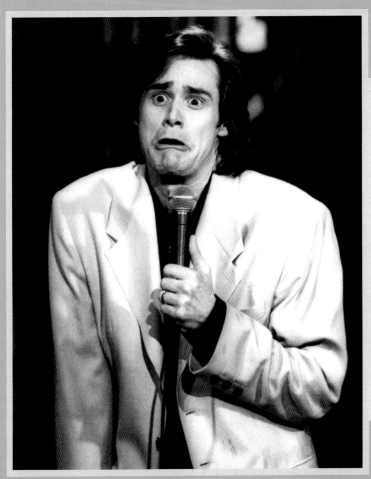

The Jim Carrey face and gestures — even without the jokes — can make audiences laugh. At the Comedy Store in 1992, Jim shows the wild-eyed, big-mouth looks that have helped make him famous.

A holiday favorite, *How the Grinch Stole Christmas* stars Jim Carrey as the Grinch. The film is based on a children's book by Dr. Seuss.

Dr. Seuss's wife loved Jim's acting. She asked Jim to use his voice for the cartoon character Horton in the upcoming movie *Horton Hears a Who*. It, too, is based on a famous book by Dr. Seuss.

same name by Dr. Seuss. In 1966, a twenty-minute cartoon, also based on the book, came out. In 2000, Jim and the filmmakers had their work cut out for them. They had to turn the story into a full-length movie. Plus, Jim had to turn the Grinch into a character that fans would want to watch for hours, not just minutes. As usual, Jim succeeded. *How the Grinch Stole Christmas* earned rave reviews from adults and children alike. It made more than $200 million. Television networks play it nearly every Christmas season.

It took Jim Carrey years of hard work to become a comic and an actor. His early training, however, began at home, in front of his family.

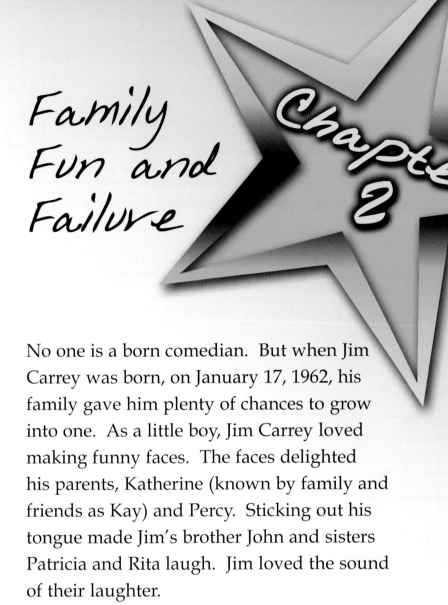

Family Fun and Failure

Chapter 2

No one is a born comedian. But when Jim Carrey was born, on January 17, 1962, his family gave him plenty of chances to grow into one. As a little boy, Jim Carrey loved making funny faces. The faces delighted his parents, Katherine (known by family and friends as Kay) and Percy. Sticking out his tongue made Jim's brother John and sisters Patricia and Rita laugh. Jim loved the sound of their laughter.

The Carreys lived in a small town about 30 miles (48 kilometers) north of Toronto, Canada. Jim's dad worked as a bookkeeper. He had dreamed of becoming a saxophone player. Jobs for musicians, however, paid too poorly to support a growing family. During his childhood, Jim noticed that his father's moods would change. Some days, his father seemed on top of the world. Other days, he seemed sad about dreams he had given up.

Jim's mother, Kay, had her own problems. Her own parents had always drunk heavily. Their alcoholism triggered depression for Kay. Jim wanted to help. "I remember having this actual thought when I was seven or eight years old," says Jim. "I'm going to prove to my mother that I'm a miracle and her life is worth something."

As an older child, Jim felt it was his job to make his parents — and his siblings — happy, if only for a few minutes. He played the role of a family clown. To become one, he spent hours in front of the mirror. He perfected goofy expressions. He also taught himself to make faces and body gestures that made him look like entertainers he admired, such as Elvis Presley and John Wayne.

Problems at Home
Jim's home life was rocky. His mother, Kay, often suffered from minor illnesses.

Jim Discovers His Destiny

One day, while her third-grade students were supposed to be listening to music, Jim's teacher saw Jim pretending to play a violin. "Jim," she said, "why don't you play for all of us?" She didn't think he would. But Jim ran to the front of the classroom. There, he pretended to be The Three Stooges, first acting as one character and then as another. (The Three Stooges, a group of popular movie and TV comedians who Jim admired, were famous for their slapstick style.) The teacher loved his act. She invited him to perform for the entire school at the upcoming Christmas program. Dressed as Santa, Jim again played The Three Stooges. When Jim finished, the whole school broke into applause. "Jim Carrey will grow up to become a comedian," the principal predicted.

Born and raised in Canada, Jim won a sidewalk star in Canada's Walk of Fame in 2004. His daughter Jane holds Jim's hand while they celebrate the unveiling of his star.

Even when she was well, she feared getting sick. She would often stay in bed for days or weeks at a time. When Jim's grandparents visited the Carrey family, they drank too much. They treated Jim's dad unkindly.

In spite of these problems, Jim felt fairly good about himself as he entered his teen years. He had confidence. He still dreamed of becoming a comedian. Percy urged Jim to perform at Toronto's first comedy club, the Yuk Yuk Komedy Kabaret. Feeling very nervous, fourteen-year-old Jim walked onstage one night in 1976 and gave it a try. He bombed. His jokes weren't right for the young adult audience. His impressions didn't make people laugh. This public failure made Jim feel terrible.

A few months later, Percy lost his bookkeeping job. Kay had been a full-time homemaker and did not hold a paying job. Eventually, Percy found work as a security guard at a factory. Oddly, the owner agreed to give

Fact File

Jim Carrey's childhood friends nicknamed him "Jimmy Gene the String Bean." Gene stands for Eugene, his middle name. And, for his age, Jim was tall and thin — like a string bean.

Percy the job only if his family worked in the factory, too — on the eight-hour night shift. In exchange, the owner let the family live in a farmhouse next to the factory.

All night long, the children who still lived at home (Pat, John, and Jim) worked in the factory. Kay ran the household. Jim went to school by day and worked at night — five nights a week. He washed, waxed, and polished the bathroom floors. He cleaned the toilets. The work left him feeling too tired to do well in school. When he turned sixteen, Jim Carrey quit school.

Working at a factory was so hard that the family quit in early 1978. With no jobs and no place to live, they moved into a rundown camper van. They were homeless. To this day, Jim finds memories of these jobless, homeless times very painful.

Slowly, the Carrey family got back on its feet. Percy, John, Pat, and Jim found new jobs. The family moved into a house, and Kay could keep being a stay-at-home mom. Jim's dream of being a comedian had disappeared for a time, but now it returned. He started practicing his impressions again.

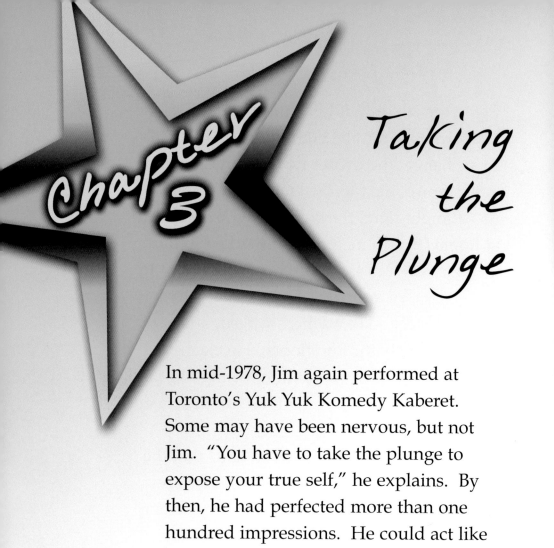

Chapter 3

Taking the Plunge

In mid-1978, Jim again performed at
Toronto's Yuk Yuk Komedy Kaberet.
Some may have been nervous, but not
Jim. "You have to take the plunge to
expose your true self," he explains. By
then, he had perfected more than one
hundred impressions. He could act like
one hundred different people! This time,
his hard work paid off. Right away, Jim
wowed his audience. People laughed.
They loved his stories and impressions.
Jim Carrey soon made a name for himself
in Toronto. A talented new comedian had
entered the entertainment scene!

Jim's work soon caught the attention
of a well-known stand-up comic, Rodney
Dangerfield. Dangerfield admired Jim.

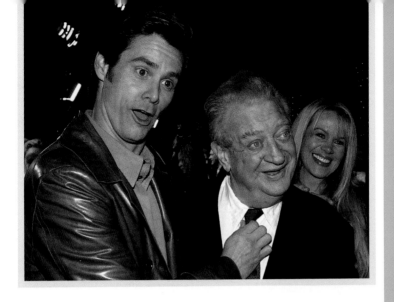

He liked that Jim never held back, always putting everything he had into his performances. Dangerfield figured that that Jim's talents could make his own comedy routine even more popular. In 1980, he invited Jim to tour with him. For several years, Dangerfield and Jim played in comedy clubs throughout Canada.

After a few years of touring, Jim began making a lot of money. He could have stayed a stand-up comic for the rest of his life. Jim, however, had bigger dreams. He wanted to break into television or even the movies. Should he go after his dreams, he wondered? Thinking about his dad gave Jim his answer. His dad had given up his

Fact File

To relax after his comedy club performances in the late 1970s, Jim played Monopoly. His friends remember him as the best Monopoly player they had ever met.

dreams for the sake of his family. Jim respected his dad for that choice. But he knew it made his father sad. Jim didn't want to turn into a broken-hearted man who had let go of his dreams. So, he moved to Los Angeles, California, where he knew that movie producers looked for new talent. He started performing at The Comedy Store.

The crowds in Los Angeles liked Jim's comedy club performances. It didn't take him long to make a name for himself. As he worked, Jim learned how to change his act during a performance. He had figured out how to "read" a crowd, or understand what they liked. Soon, he reached another turning point in his career: He stopped doing impressions. Other comics told him he was crazy. "Why stop doing the thing that makes you famous," they asked? The answer was that too many other comics did impressions of other people. Jim wanted to stand out with his own brand of humor.

Jim started taking acting classes in the late 1980s. He studied other great

Hot Comedy

In Living Color played on television nearly twenty years ago. Some Jim Carrey fans, however, still remember such Jim Carrey parts as Fire Marshall Bill. While teaching fire "safety," Bill would accidentally set himself on fire. Some adults worried that young viewers would take the terrible "safety" tips seriously. They feared that kids would try to imitate the fire marshall and hurt themselves. When real fire marshalls would teach safety to school students, during the early 1990s, many students would yell: "We want Fire Marshall Bill!"

By playing Fire Marshall Bill, Jim helped make the TV comedy *In Living Color* a huge hit. His over-sized hat and silly grin made him look like a fire marshall who would start a fire rather than put one out.

comedians. He decided to add more physical humor to his act. He might flop around on the stage, pretending to be a worm. At first, people hated his new act. "People would be screaming at me to do my old act, and actually be violent and angry at me," Jim said. But soon, his fans came around. People began to see Jim Carrey as more than a stand-up joke teller.

In 1984, Jim's hard work began to pay off. He earned a starring role in the NBC television program *The Duck Factory*. The show lasted only one season. It did, however, give Jim a chance to expand his comedy talents.

In 1988, Jim won a small role in the movie *Earth Girls Are Easy*. He didn't even have any lines. But his comedy impressed his co-star Damon Wayans. Damon's brother, Keenan Ivory

Fact File

Jim tried out for a part on *Saturday Night Live* in 1980. On the way into the studio he spotted an NBC worker on top of the roof. The man was about to jump. Jim says the sight so upset him, he performed poorly during the try-out.

Wayans, created a television show for a new network called FOX, in 1990. Damon convinced Keenan to give Jim a part. For several years, Jim helped make *In Living Color* an outstanding comedy. Like *Saturday Night Live, In Living Color* featured sketch comedy, which is actors appearing in skits or brief stories. Unlike *Saturday Night Live, In Living Color* featured only African American actors — except for Jim. His sketches led to a film role in *Ace Ventura: Pet Detective.* The movie made Jim a superstar.

In Living Color broke barriers in 1990 by casting almost all African American comics. In the series' first season, Jim was the only white actor. His outstanding talent — and friendship with the producer's brother — had won him a role.

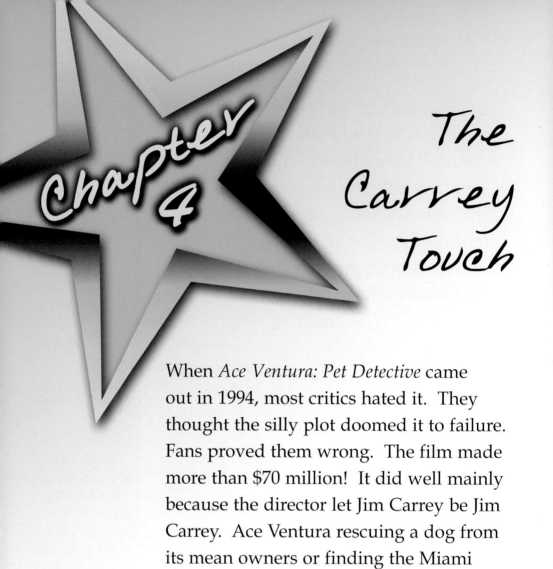

Chapter 4

The Carrey Touch

When *Ace Ventura: Pet Detective* came out in 1994, most critics hated it. They thought the silly plot doomed it to failure. Fans proved them wrong. The film made more than $70 million! It did well mainly because the director let Jim Carrey be Jim Carrey. Ace Ventura rescuing a dog from its mean owners or finding the Miami Dolphin's missing dolphin doesn't sound funny. But the Jim Carrey touch — wild eyes, huge grin, rubbery body, and a willingness to act like a fool — made viewers laugh. After *Ace Ventura*, the Hollywood studios knew that Jim's out-of-control style could make them money. They offered him more roles. In 1994, Jim also starred in *The Mask*

Checking His Success

At Percy Carrey's funeral, Jim put a $10 million check in Percy's pocket. Years earlier, Jim had written the check to himself. At the time, it was worthless — Jim did not have $10 million in the bank. He hoped that someday he would have that much money. The check was a symbol of his wish for success. By the time his father died, Jim had finally made it. He left the check with his father. Doing so reminded Jim that his father had shared his dream of success and believed in him. Even though Percy had given up his own dream of becoming a musician, he had helped his son achieve his dream. Jim wanted his father to have the check.

and *Dumb and Dumber*. Each new movie made more money than the last.

In *The Mask*, Jim played the mild-mannered Stanley Ipkis. But when Stanley put on a magic mask, he turned into a superhero (*right*). The movie makers had planned to using a mask that covered Jim's face. But when they discovered Jim's range of facial expressions, they built a special mask. It let his expressions show through. The director said that Jim's talent saved them

Fact File

a lot of money. Had they used another actor, less skilled in making wild facial expressions, they would have needed a far more costly mask.

Success gave Jim money to spend — and lots of it. In 1994, he paid $4 million for a mansion. He bought his dream car, a 1965 robin's-egg-blue Thunderbird. Career success, however, did not always lead to personal success. Jim spent so much time working, he had little time left for his wife, Melissa Womer. They divorced in 1995.

Jim's father, Percy, died in 1994 from cancer. Of course, Jim felt sad. He had loved his father very much. He also felt regret. Despite Jim's success, he had never been able to make his father a truly happy man. His father had suffered too much bad luck and too many broken dreams.

During the 1994 filming of *Dumb and Dumber*, Jim fell in love with co-star Lauren Holly. They married not long after finishing the movie. Sadly, the marriage ended in divorce within a year.

Same Old Same Old

Once they have won fame and earned a fortune, many actors make the same kinds of movies — over and over. But playing the same kinds of roles bored Jim. So, he decided to take a risk. In 1998, he broke away from comedy roles.

He took on his first serious role in the movie *The Truman Show*. Jim played Truman Burbank, an ordinary man who went about his daily life. He didn't know that hidden cameras taped his every move. His life was a TV

Fact File

In *Dumb and Dumber*, Jim's character, Lloyd, had a chipped front tooth. Jim Carrey really has a chipped front tooth. He keeps it covered with a dental cap. For his role as Lloyd, Jim decided to remove it. He used his own chipped tooth to make Lloyd look goofy.

show watched by hundreds of thousands of viewers!

Although *The Truman Show* had some funny moments, it was basically a serious movie. *The Truman Show* producers were not sure if Jim's fans would like him in a serious role. They did. *The Truman Show* made over $100 million and Jim won a Golden Globe Best Actor award for his performance. He was starting to prove that he is more than just a wild comedian.

In 2006, Jim won the most sought-after annual MTV Movie Award, the "Generation Award." With a flock of angels behind him, Jim expresses his thanks.

The Many Sides of Jim Carrey

In between playing comedy roles, Jim now fills dramatic parts. The comedies have made more money at the box office. But the serious roles have become an important part of Jim's career. They have earned him the respect of moviegoers and critics. Fans and moviemakers alike believe that Jim Carrey is a serious actor as well as a comedian.

Many of his fans enjoyed his performance in the 2000 comedy *Me, Myself and Irene*. Jim played a man with two personalities. One is a kind and helpful police officer. He tries to help Irene escape from a corrupt ex-boyfriend. He remains calm — in part, because of medicine that keeps him that way. When the police officer loses his medicine, the other personality appears. Of course, the

other personality is wacky and out of control. Fans watched Jim swing from a calm, nice guy into a raving madman in the same movie — sometimes during the same scene.

Playing Quiet and Shy

In 2004, Jim starred in *Eternal Sunshine of the Spotless Mind.* He played a quiet and shy man named Joel Barish. The movie did not make a lot of money. It did show, however, that Jim could stretch himself as an actor. In this movie, Jim earned the respect of many critics.

In his second role of 2004, Jim played the evil Count Olaf in *Lemony Snicket's A Series of Unfortunate Events.* Children, young adults, and even adults liked it. Count Olaf, who looks after the three young children, is actually trying to steal the children's fortune. It gave Jim a chance, once again, to turn himself into a character from a beloved book.

Fact File

Lots of successful movie stars have started their careers with stand-up comedy. Stars such as Adam Sandler, Robin Williams, Will Ferrell, and Eddie Murphy, all began as stand-up comics.

The 2007 movie *The Number 23* gave Jim a chance to star in a suspenseful thriller. He played Walter Sparrow, a dog catcher who reads a mysterious book called *The Number 23*. Sparrow becomes convinced that the book is about his life. Everything that happens in the book, he believes, will happen in his life. The book ends with a murder that Sparrow tries to prevent. The movie showed that Carrey is never afraid to try a new kind of role.

Jim Carrey is hugely successful in large part because he works at it. He also takes care of himself. "I'm very serious about no alcohol. No drugs," Jim says. "Life is too beautiful." Along with this dedication to his work, family and friends are important to Jim. He enjoys spending time with his grown daughter Jane. He is also in love again: Jim has been dating actor/model Jenny McCarthy since the summer of 2006. "Jen's a sweetheart. . . " says Jim, "and I am more ready to be loved than I have been in my life."

In *The Number 23*, Jim plays two characters in one movie: the dog catcher Walter Sparrow and a sleazy detective in the book Walter is reading.

Giving Back

Becoming rich and famous has given Jim a chance to help others. He has supported many charities. For years, he donated to Comic Relief, a charity that helps homeless people. Because of his family's experience with homelessness, this charity means a lot to him. He has served as honorary chairman for the National Veterans Foundation. He has also given money to the Luke Neuhedel Foundation that aids kids with cancer. His donations to the Toy Mountain Campaign help many poor children receive toys, food, and clothes during the winter holiday season.

Jim has come a long way from a childhood marked by family problems. He withstood the tough years of stand-up comedy to make a big name for himself as a serious actor and a comedian. He has fulfilled many of his dreams. His talents now entertain fans around the world.

Fact File

Sometimes, Jim Carrey will write "Have a good day!" on $20 bills. Then, he drops the bills on park benches and other public places. He doesn't stick around to see the reaction of those who find the money. He just wants to brighten up someone's day. He knows that everyone enjoys finding money.

Time Line

1962	James Eugene Carrey is born in Canada.
1976	First performs at Canada's Yuk Yuk Komedy Kabaret Club.
1980s	Performs in Los Angeles. Starts touring with comedian Rodney Dangerfield.
1987	Marries Melissa Womer (and divorces in 1995).
1990	Stars in seven episodes of *In Living Color*, through 1994.
1994	Becomes star in *Ace Ventura: Pet Detective*.
1996	Marries Lauren Holly but divorces within a year.
1998	Plays a serious role in *The Truman Show*.
1999	Wins a Golden Globe Award for Best Actor Performance in *Man on the Moon*.
2004	Stars in *Eternal Sunshine of the Spotless Mind*.
2007	Stars in the movie *The Number 23*.

Glossary

accidentally — when something happens by chance

character — a person played by an actor in a film

corrupt — dishonest

expressions — looks on a person's face that show, or *express*, emotions

gestures — motions of a person's limbs or body that show thoughts and feelings

impressions — humorous imitations of a famous person's voice or mannerisms

mansion — a very large house

miracle — a good event for which there is no known cause

mysterious — not well understood or explainable

range — a wide variety of styles

routine — a comedy act that includes jokes and impressions

skits — comedy acts that tell short stories

To Find Out More

Books

Funny Bones: Comedy Games and Activities. Lisa Bany-
  Winters (Chicago Review Press, Inc.)

Jim Carrey: Funny Man. Joan Wallner (Abdo)

Jim Carrey. Mary Hughes (Chelsea House Publishers)

Jim Carrey. John F. Wukovits (Lucent Books Inc.)

Web Sites

Comedy skills for kids
www.kidkomedy.com
Clean comedy with educational, entertainment, and
product offerings.

Official Grinch movie
www.grinched.com
Enter Whoville for an online tour of the Grinch's world.

Official Lemony Snicket movie site
www.unfortunateeventsmovie.com
Proceed with curiosity — and caution! — into this
complex site of "unfortunate events."

Publisher's note to educators and parents: Our editors have carefully
reviewed these Web sites to ensure that they are suitable for children.
Many Web sites change frequently, however, and we cannot guarantee
that a site's future contents will continue to meet our high standards
of quality and educational value. Be advised that children should be
closely supervised whenever they access the Internet.

Index

About the Author

Author Amy Stone likes writing about famous people. Many of her eleven nonfiction books have focused on famous women and men, such as Jim Carrey. "It's fascinating," she says, "to see how people use their talents to enrich the world." Her two children are grown, but they still help her write the books. They let her know if the rough drafts make sense and hold interest. She hopes that this book provides insight about determination. For Jim Carrey, determination led to success.